MY FIRST REFERENCE LIBRARY

ANIMALS

BELITHA PRESS

First published in Great Britain in 1990 by
Belitha Press Limited
31 Newington Green, London N16 9PU

ISBN 1 85561 021 3
Typeset by Chambers Wallace, London
Printed in the UK for Imago Publishing
by MacLehose and Partners

British Library Cataloguing in Publication Data
CIP data for this book is available from the British Library

Acknowledgements

Photographic credits:

Bruce Coleman 26, 36 right, 37, 52
Frank Lane 15, 18 right, 25, 30, 32, 33, 34, 36 left, 38, 40, 43, 45, 46, 48, 49, 53, 55, 56, 57, 58 left, 59
NHPA 27
Natural Science Photos 18 left, 19 right
Oxford Scientific Films 31, 39
Planet Earth 9, 58 right

Illustrated by: Adam Abel, Teresa O'Brien, Eric Robson, Roger Walker and Lorna Turpin

This book is based on an original text by: Steve Pollock

Series editor: Neil Champion
Educational consultant: Carolyn Kain
Editorial: Dee Turner and Kate Scarborough
Designed by: Groom and Pickerill
Picture research and art editing: Ann Usborne
Specialist consultant: the late Dr Gwynne Vevers

Contents

Words found in **bold** are explained in the glossary on pages 60 and 61

CHAPTER ONE

ANIMAL LIFE

The Animal Kingdom

Lions, tigers, birds, bees and fishes are all animals. Humans are animals too. Some animals are so small that you would need a magnifying glass to see them.

Almost every place in the world has some animal life. Different kinds of creatures live in the oceans, forests, deserts and mountains.

Animals gradually change, or adapt, to suit their living conditions. Penguins, for example, are birds whose wings have become flippers. This has

happened because penguins need to swim to catch fish in the sea. Major changes like this take place over thousands of years.

Species of animals

Scientists have found about one million different kinds, or species, of animals. And more **species** are discovered each year. The scientists often find new kinds of animals in **tropical** forests. But the people in some countries are cutting down their forests and allowing many animals to die out. So we shall never know how many species lived there.

Facts and feats

- The giant squid can grow to over 18 metres long.
- A flock of whooper swans were seen flying at a height of over 8,000 metres. This is almost as high as Mount Everest, the highest mountain in the world.
- The animal that lives the longest is the tortoise. One particular tortoise lived for at least 152 years.
- Arctic terns migrate from the Arctic, where they breed, to the Antarctic. Once a year they do a round trip of 40,000 kilometres (25,000 miles).

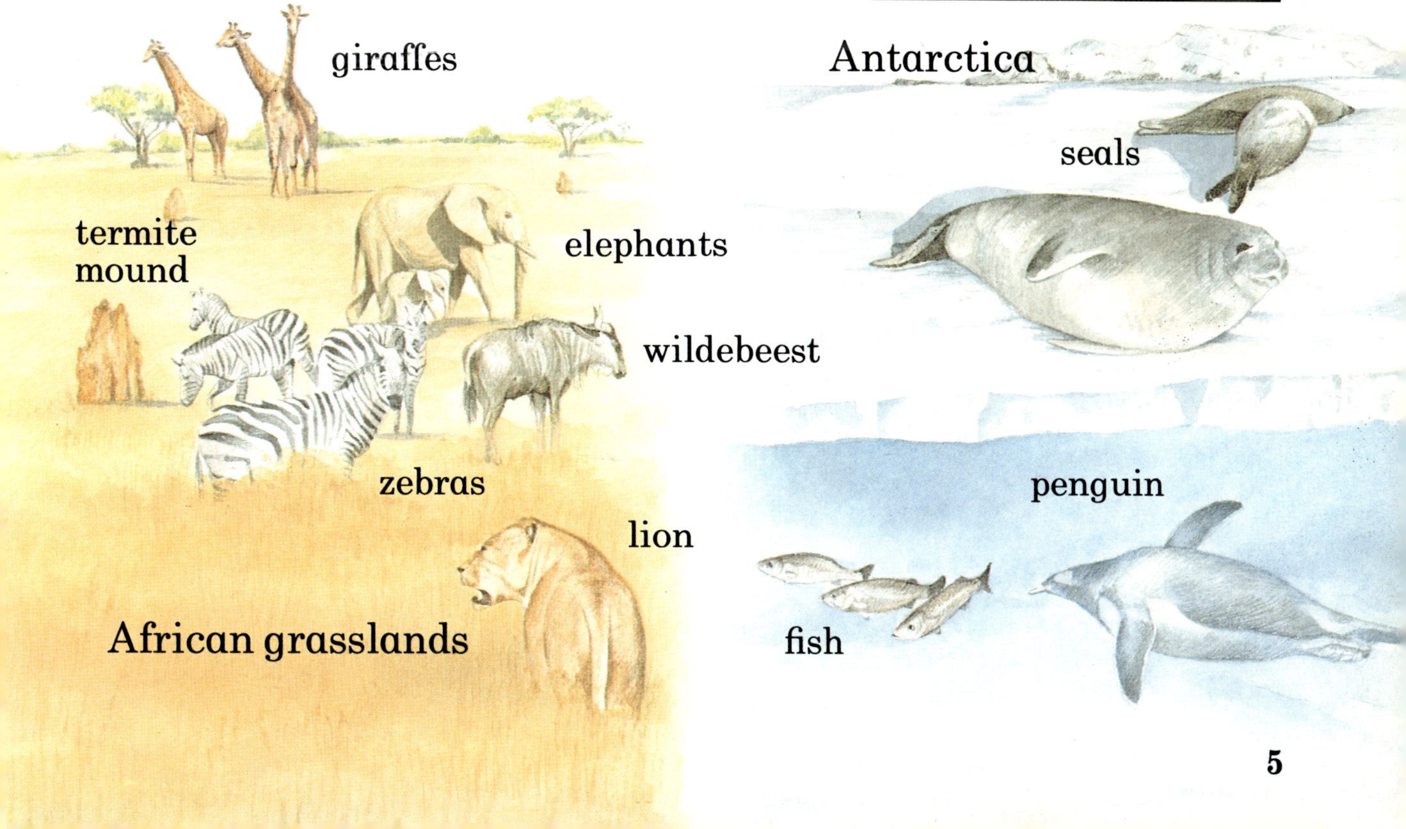

1
The lion shares certain features with other big cats. They all roar, and lie with their front feet stretched out. They never fold them like the domestic cat does. All the big cats are put together in the same group, called the GENUS *Panthera*.

Animal Groups

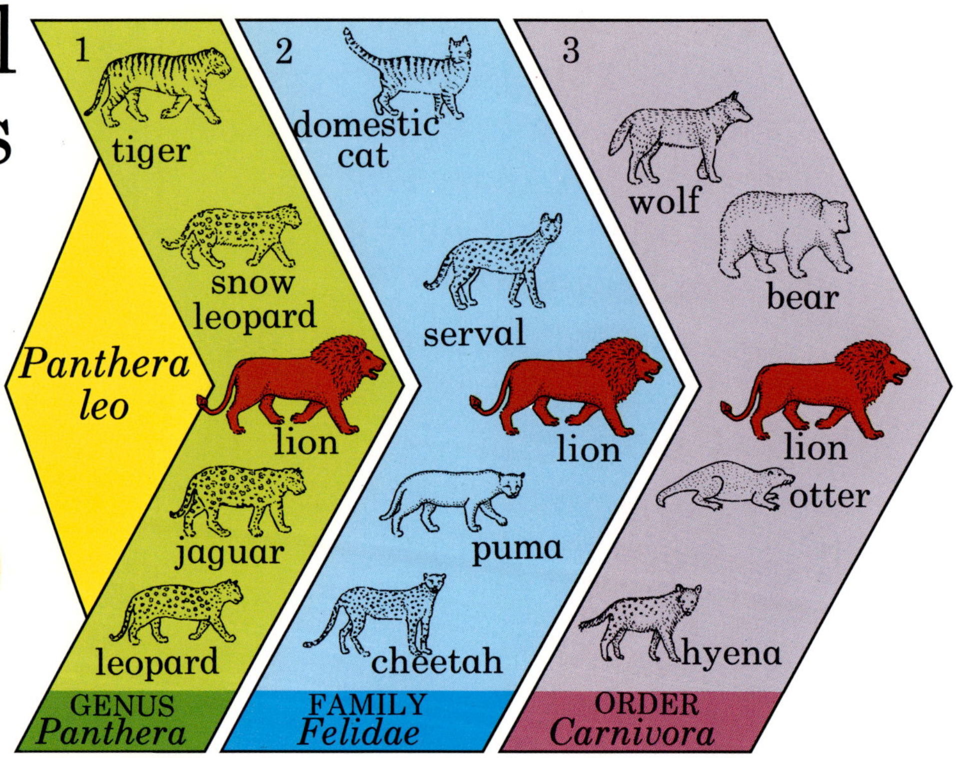

▲ It is quite easy to tell a lion from other animals. It has certain features that no other animals have. So we call the lion a SPECIES. All lions belong to the same species. Biologists give the lion the Latin name, *Panthera leo*. *Leo* means lion, and *Panthera* is the name of the animal group that it belongs to.

2
The big cats and small cats have some features in common. Both groups belong to the cat FAMILY, which is called *Felidae*.

3
All members of the cat, dog, bear, hyena, weasel and racoon families are meat eaters. Such families all belong to the ORDER of animals called *Carnivora*.

4

All orders of animals that have hair, give birth to live young and feed them on milk are called mammals. These orders belong to the CLASS called *Mammalia*.

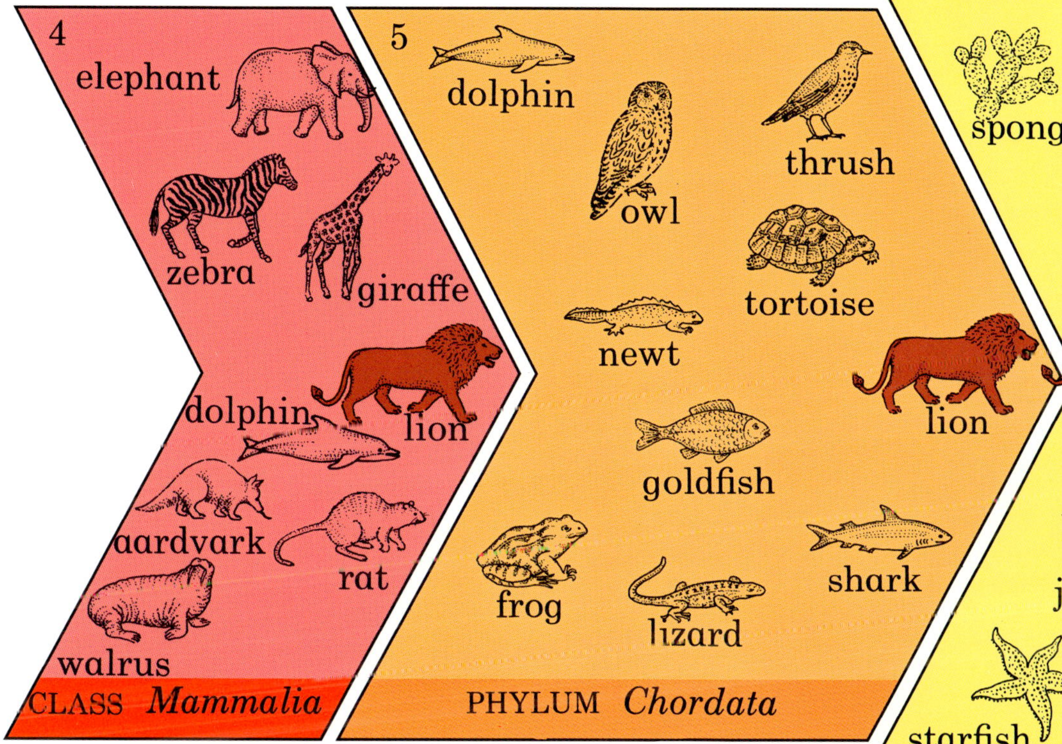

5

The next group is called a PHYLUM. The mammals and all other classes of animals with backbones belong to the phylum called *Chordata*.

6

All the phyla of animals belong to one group. This is called the Animal KINGDOM, or *Animalia*.

Evolution

The first animals on Earth appeared in the oceans about 1,000 million years ago. These were small, simple forms of life. Some gradually changed over millions of years to form more complex animals. This process of change is called **evolution**.

All the creatures that have lived on the Earth were formed in this way. Some sea animals moved

Tyrannosaurus rex

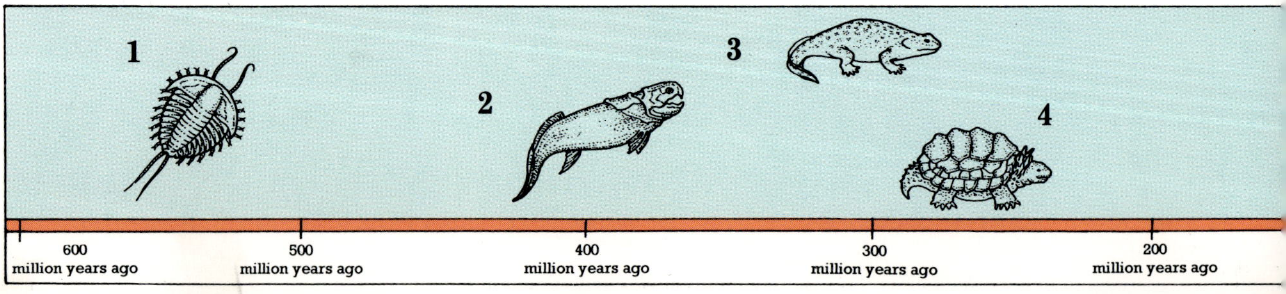

onto the land. Some of these eventually developed wings and started to fly.

Dinosaurs

The first dinosaurs appeared about 240 million years ago. For about 170 million years, dinosaurs lived on the Earth. Then they suddenly died out.

Fossils

Scientists have learnt much about evolution from **fossils**. These are traces of past life forms. They have been preserved in ancient rocks.

Living fossils

▲ Some animals have stayed unchanged for millions of years. We call these 'living fossils'. Scientists thought that the coelacanth had been extinct for 70 million years. So they were amazed when one was caught in 1938.

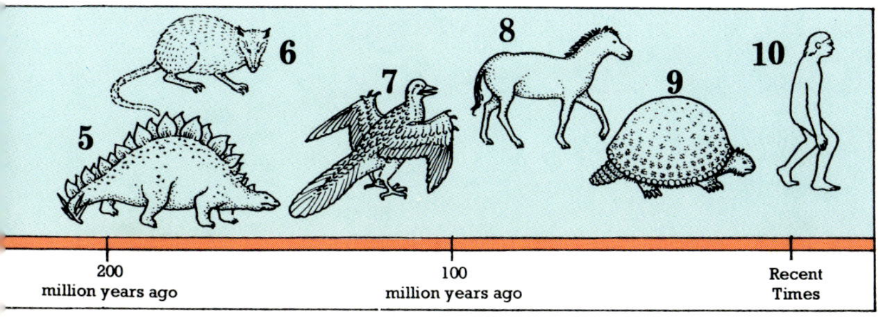

▶ This time chart shows when various forms of animal life appeared on the Earth.

1 *Trilobita* (arthropod)
2 *Placodermi* (fish)
3 *Seymouria* (amphibian)
4 *Chelonia* (turtle)
5 *Stegosaurus* (dinosaur)
6 *Pantothere* (mammal)
7 *Archaeopteryx* (bird)
8 *Perissodactyla* (horse)
9 *Glyptodon* (armadillo)
10 *Homo habilis* (early human)

Breathing

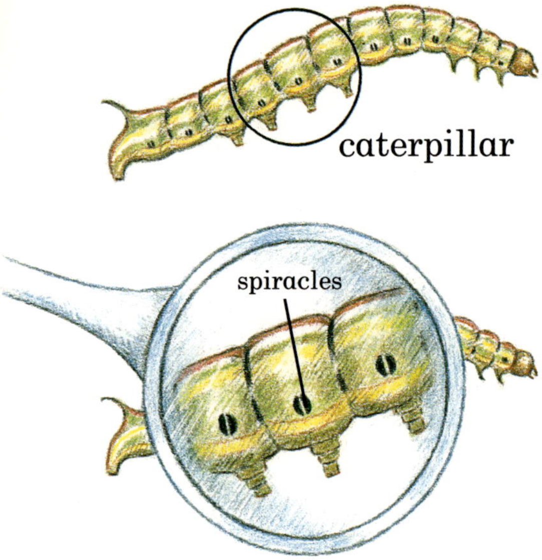

▲ An insect breathes through holes, called spiracles, in the sides of its body.

In order to live, all animals must breathe in oxygen gas and breathe out waste carbon dioxide gas. Some animals breathe oxygen from the air. Others breathe oxygen from the water.

Air breathers

Air breathers, such as insects, birds and **mammals**, get oxygen from the air they breathe. An earthworm breathes through its skin. This process is called diffusion. Larger animals have lungs.

In the lungs, oxygen from the air

Did you know?

The lungfish from Africa can breathe under the water and in air. When the lakes dry up, lungfish burrow into the mud and cover themselves with slime.

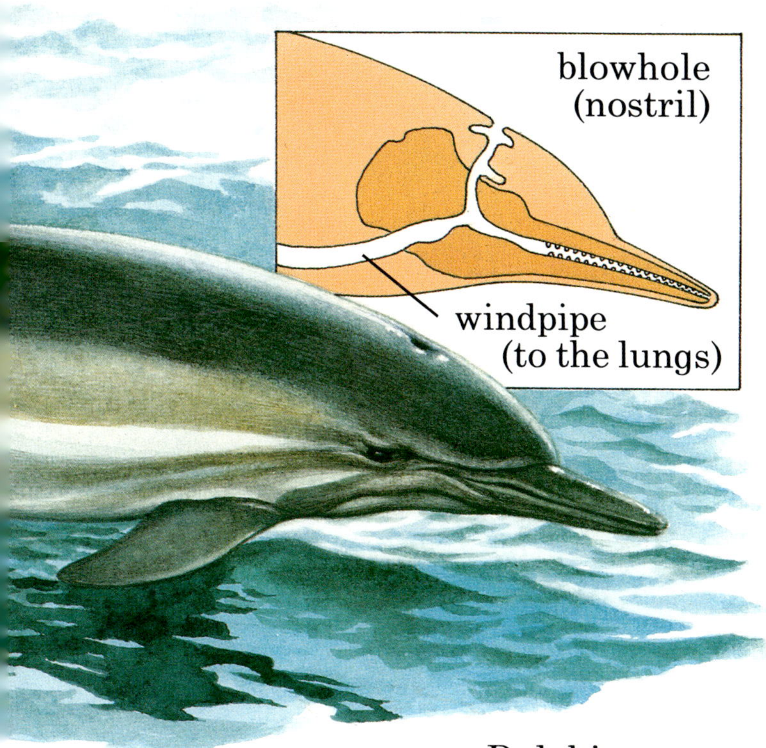

Dolphin

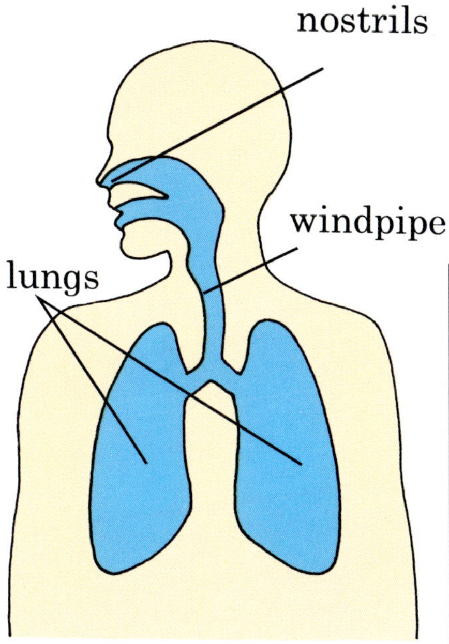

▲ People breathe using lungs. Air passes in and out of the body through the nostrils.

passes into the blood. The blood carries the oxygen around the body. The lungs also take up waste carbon dioxide from the blood. This gas is breathed out.

Water breathers
Fishes breathe under water using gills. These **organs** do the same as lungs, but they work in water instead of air.

Some animals live in water but breathe air. The dolphin, for example, is an air breathing **mammal**. On top of its head is a nostril called a blowhole.

▼ A fish breathes by taking water in through its mouth. It passes the water over its gills. These take up oxygen that is dissolved in the water.

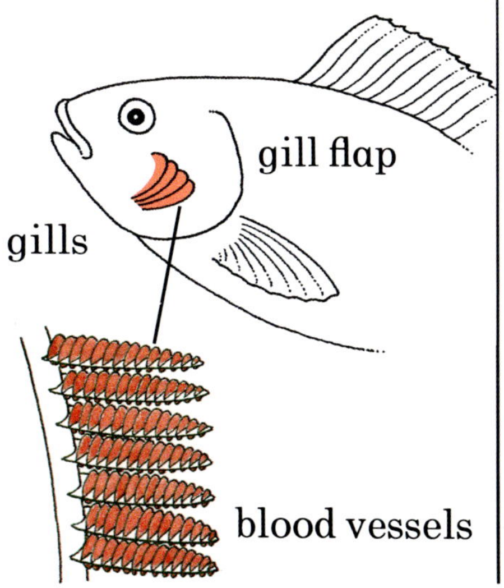

Body Heat

Warm-blooded animals have warm body temperatures that don't change much. Cold-blooded animals have body temperatures that change with the temperature around them.

Birds and **mammals**, including humans, are warm-blooded. Birds have feathers, and most mammals have hair or fur to help keep heat in their bodies. Cold-blooded animals include fishes, **reptiles** and insects. As they cannot keep their body temperature constant,

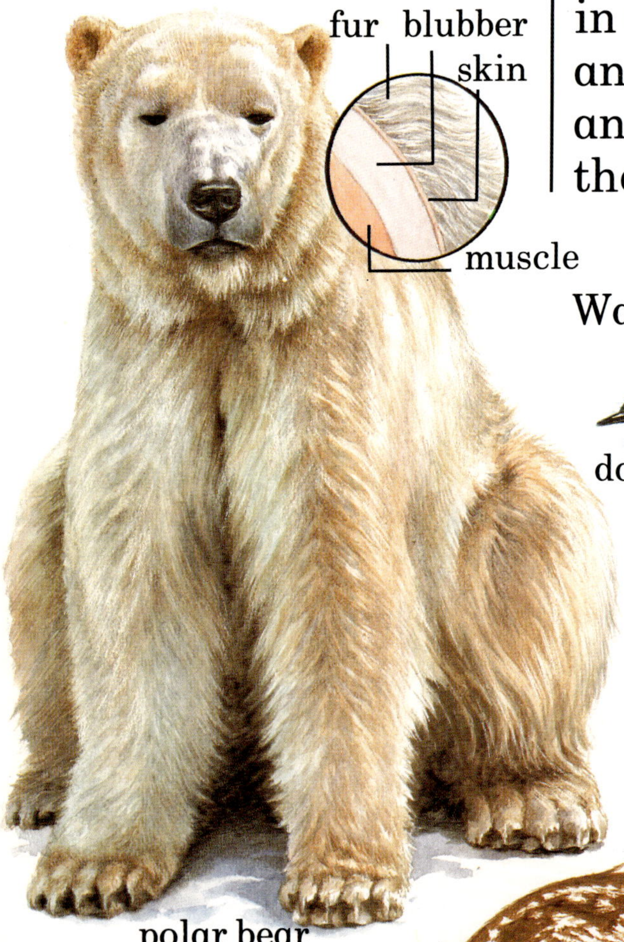

they usually avoid extreme heat or cold.

Coping with the cold

Food provides the energy that mammals need to keep warm. But food may be scarce in winter. So some mammals, such as the ground squirrel, eat a lot during the autumn. This adds fat to their bodies. When winter comes, they go into a deep sleep called **hibernation**. In this state, they need very little food. They get all they need by slowly using up their body fat.

Cold-blooded animals

- Rely on heat from the Sun to keep up their body temperature.
- Have no special skin covering to keep them warm in cold weather.
- Mostly hide away and rest during a freezing winter.

Cold-blooded animals

CHAPTER TWO

MOVEMENT

On the Land

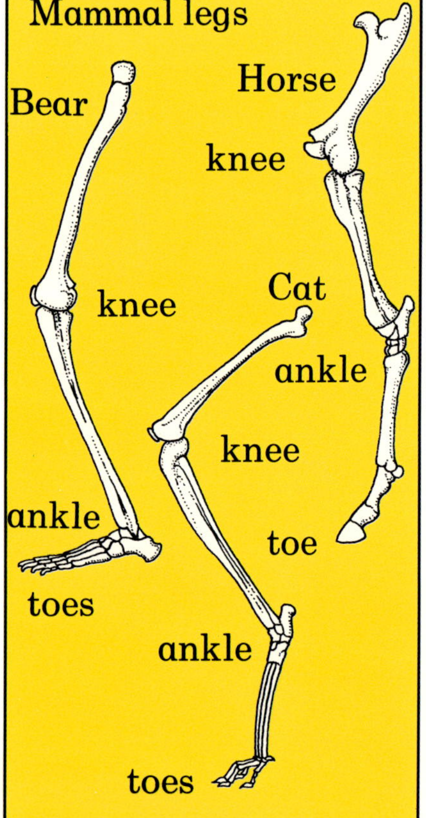

The bear puts its feet flat on the ground. The cat puts only part of its feet on the ground. And the horse stands on its toes, which we call the hooves. Faster animals touch the ground with a smaller part of the foot than slower animals.

Land mammals walk and run by using the muscles in their legs. The muscles are attached to bones in the legs and make them move. Other parts of the body may move as well so that the animal keeps its balance. The cheetah uses its long tail to help it balance. For the same reason, we move our arms when we are walking or running.

Legless animals

Although snakes have no legs,

The Cheetah

The cheetah has a bendy backbone, long legs and strong muscles.

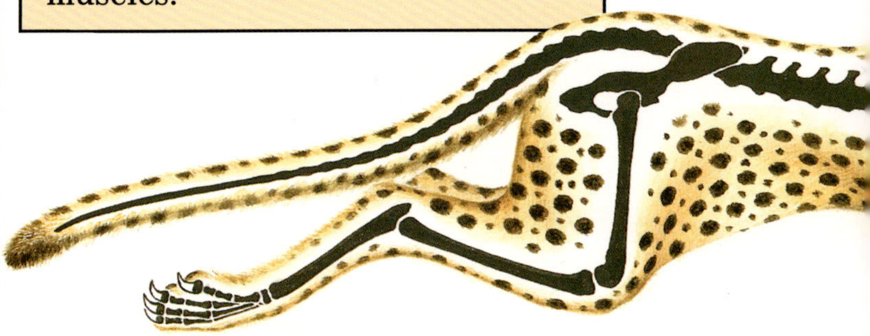

The cheetah's claws help it to grip the ground when running.

some can move quite quickly. They use muscles to wriggle their bodies along the ground.

Snails have no legs either. But they move along on a muscular foot. The muscles in the foot move one after another and slowly push the snail forward.

Runners

When we walk, our heels touch the ground. But, when we run, we touch the ground with only the front part of our feet. In many animals, the feet have developed so that only the front touches the ground. This helps them to run faster than other animals.

Ridges in the footpads grip the ground firmly.

▲ Crabs have eight legs and move sideways across the sand.

Facts and feats

- The frog that jumps furthest is the South African sharp-nosed frog. Some females can jump a distance of 3 metres.
- The black mamba is the fastest snake. It can travel at more than 11 kilometres (7 miles) per hour.
- The fastest land mammal is the cheetah. It can run at over 100 kilometres (65 miles) per hour.
- The ostrich is a bird that cannot fly. But it can run at up to 72 kilometres (45 miles) per hour.
- The common snail has a top speed of 20 metres per hour. This means that it would take a snail two days and nights to travel 1 kilometre (just over half a mile).

In the Trees

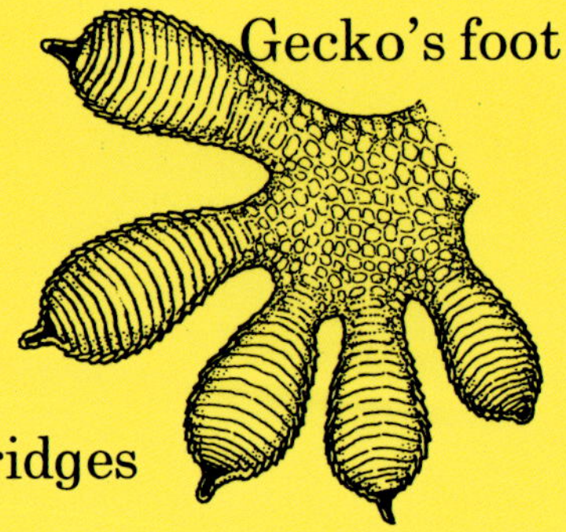

Spider monkey's tail

Did you know?

Tree frogs and some lizards can hold onto the underside of a sheet of glass. The toes have tiny ridges and hooks. These grip tightly onto surface cracks that are too small for us to see.

To move in trees without falling, an animal needs a tight grip. It must also have good eyesight and a way to balance itself.

Graspers
Humans, monkeys and apes have what is called an opposable thumb. This means that it can be placed against the fingers, making it easy to grasp objects.

Some monkeys and other tree-living animals have a **prehensile** (gripping) tail. It helps when

climbing trees. Many birds have feet suitable for gripping branches. But the woodpecker has feet that give a good grip on the trunk of a tree. This is where the woodpecker searches for insects to eat.

In the trees

Some monkeys swing through the trees, using their hands to grip the branches. Squirrels leap with their strong hind legs. They use their tail to balance the weight of their body.

In the Earth

▲ The razor shell clam uses a long, muscular foot to burrow into the sand.

► The armadillo's armour stops it getting scratched by stones.

Many animals make snug homes in the ground. Some of them find food there as well and never need to leave their burrows.

Feet and claws

The armadillo has powerful feet and claws for digging a **burrow** as much as three metres below the ground. It also uses its claws to rip open ant nests so that it can eat the ants. The largest species is the giant armadillo. The adult is about 120 cm long.

The mole also has powerful front legs. Its broad feet and big claws work like shovels to dig tunnels through the soil. The mole can move backwards through its tunnels just as easily as it can go forwards. This is useful as there may not be room to turn around.

▲ The mole and the earthworm are built very differently. But they are both experts at moving in the soil.

Tunnelling without claws

Earthworms dig their tunnels by eating the soil as they go. Tiny bristles anchor the rear end of the body to the tunnel walls, while the front end pushes forward. Then the bristles at the front end dig into the walls, while the rear end is pulled forward.

▲ The sandfish is actually a lizard. Its snake-like body helps it to 'swim' through the sand.

In the Air

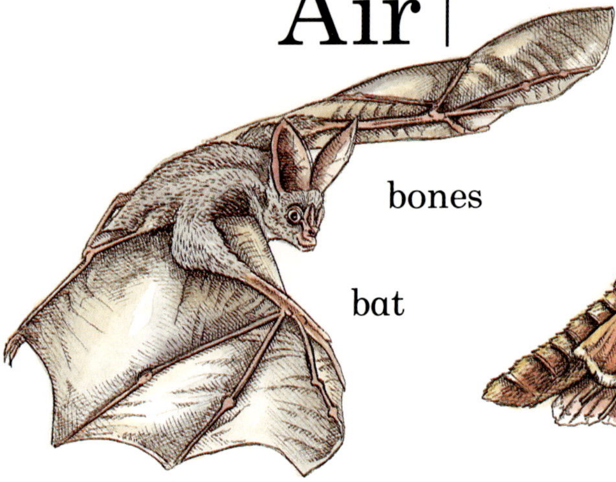

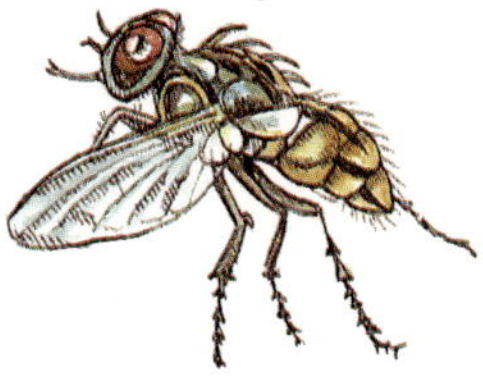

▲ Bat wings are made of skin stretched over the bones of the legs, arms and fingers. Bird wings are covered with feathers. Birds have bones that are hollow and very light.

Bats, birds and insects can all fly. They flap their broad wings to stay up in the air and to drive themselves forward.

Kinds of wings

These flying animals all have strong muscles to work their wings. Bats and birds have bones in their wings. Most insects have two pairs of thin wings that are supported by strong **veins**. Flies, however, have only one pair of delicate wings.

Did you know?

Beetles have four wings, but the two outer ones form a hard covering. They protect the two delicate flying wings.

Gliding

Flying lizards, flying frogs and flying squirrels can all glide through the air, but they can't really fly. They don't have real wings. They just have flaps of skin. These open out and keep them in the air just long enough to glide from tree to tree. Flying fish can leap from the water and glide on their big fins.

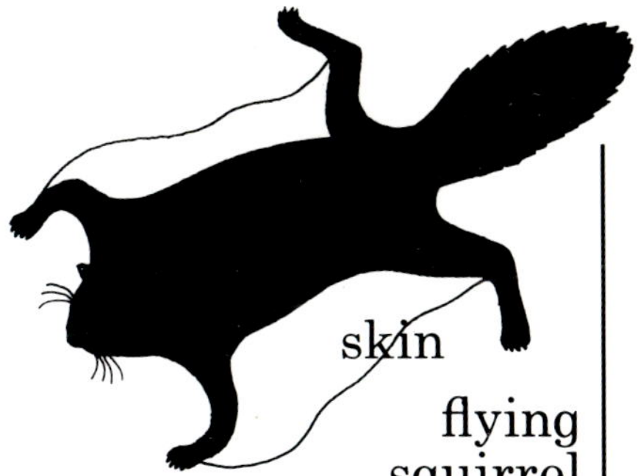

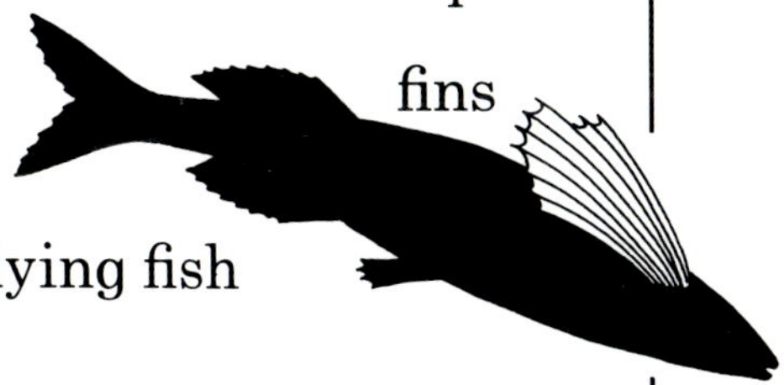

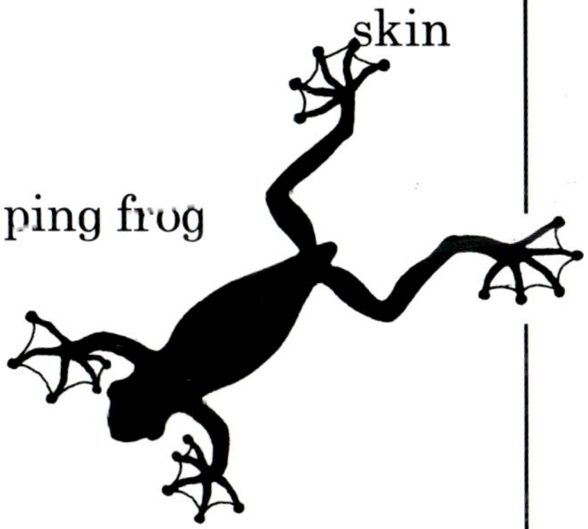

▲ All of these animals can glide through the air, but none of them can really fly.

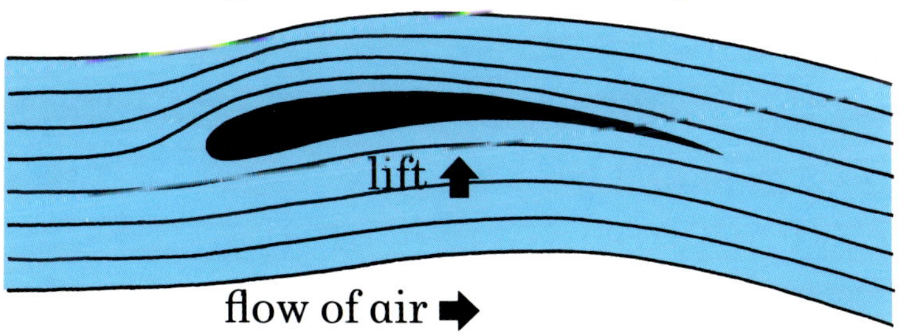

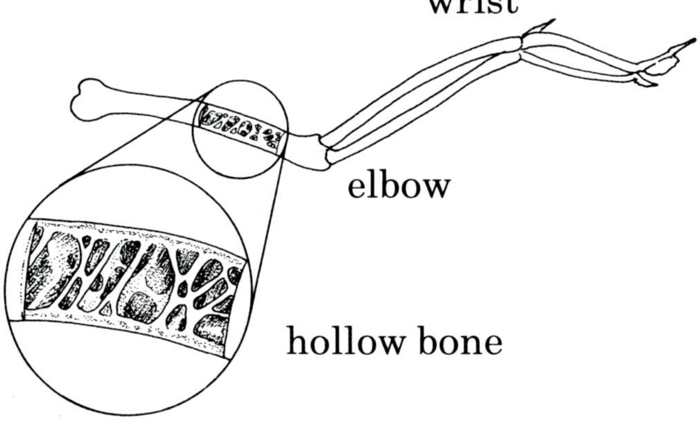

◀ Air pushing up under the curved wing of a bird helps to lift it. Having lightweight bones makes it easier for a bird to fly.

Parachuting spiders

Baby spiders can drift through the air on long strands of silk – just as if they had parachutes.

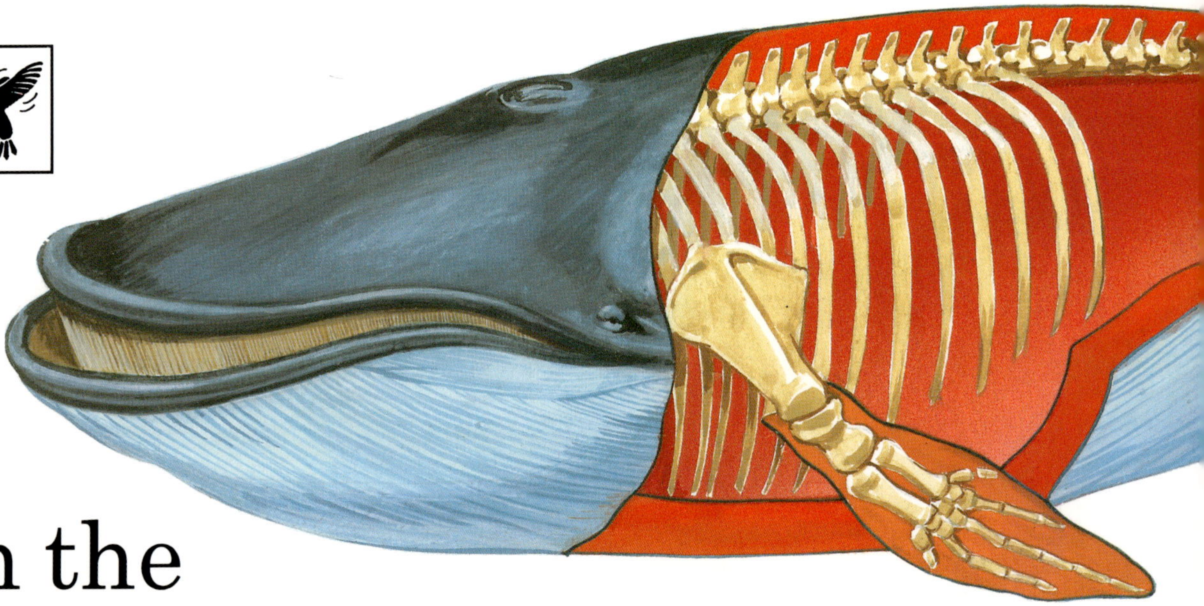

In the Water

▲ These animals all have a streamlined shape when in the water. Penguins swim with their wings and steer with their feet.

We can float in water, but not in air. Water is 800 times **denser** (thicker) than air, so it can hold us up. Although the blue whale may weigh over 130 tonnes, it can still float in water. But it would be too heavy to move about on land, even if it had legs.

Streamlining

Like most other water animals, the whale has a **streamlined** body. It is narrow at each end and wider in the middle. This helps it to move easily through the water. Millions of years ago, the whales had legs. But their front legs

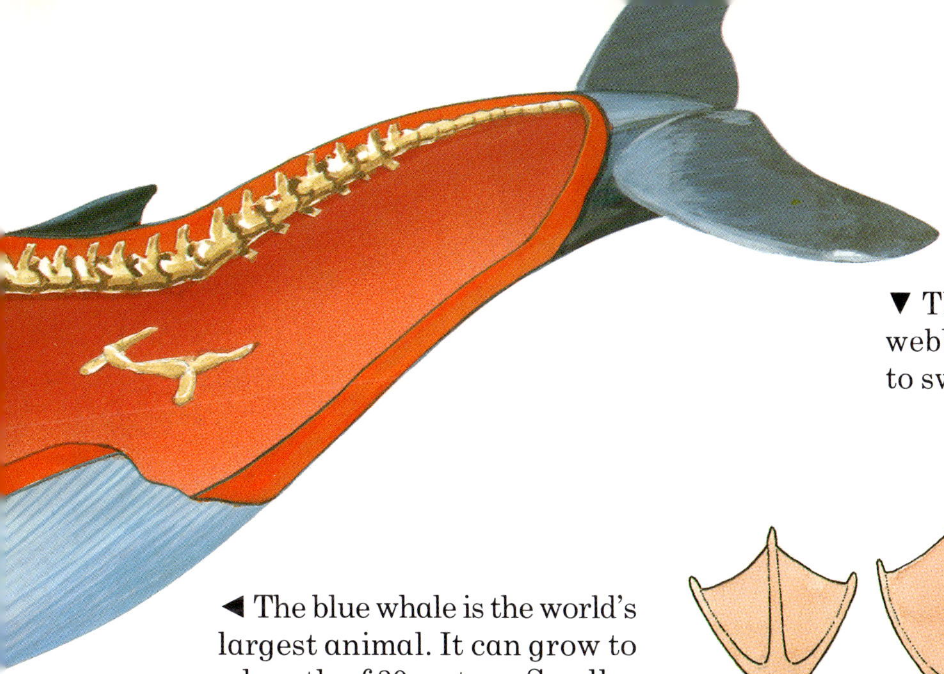

◀ The blue whale is the world's largest animal. It can grow to a length of 30 metres. Small bones near the back are all that remain of the back legs that the whale had long ago.

▼ These animals all have webbed feet to help them to swim.

gradually changed into **flippers**. Their back legs disappeared as the animals became streamlined.

Swimming

Whales, seals and most fish push themselves through the water by waving their tails. They steer with their flippers and fins. The squid swims by **jet propulsion**. It squirts out a powerful jet of water, which sends the animal zooming off in the opposite direction. Some animals, such as the frog, have webbed feet. Skin between their toes helps them to swim faster.

Facts and feats

- The fastest-swimming mammal is the killer whale. One was seen moving at over 55 kilometres (34 miles) per hour.
- The grey whale swims almost 20,000 kilometres (12,000 miles) every year. It travels down the west coast of the USA, from Alaska to California, and later returns.
- Pond skaters and other insects can walk on water. Tufts of greasy hair on their feet stop them from breaking through the surface.

CHAPTER THREE
FOOD

Predators

Predatory animals, or **predators**, kill and eat other animals, which are called **prey**. Each kind of predator has its own way of catching and killing its prey.

Super swallowers

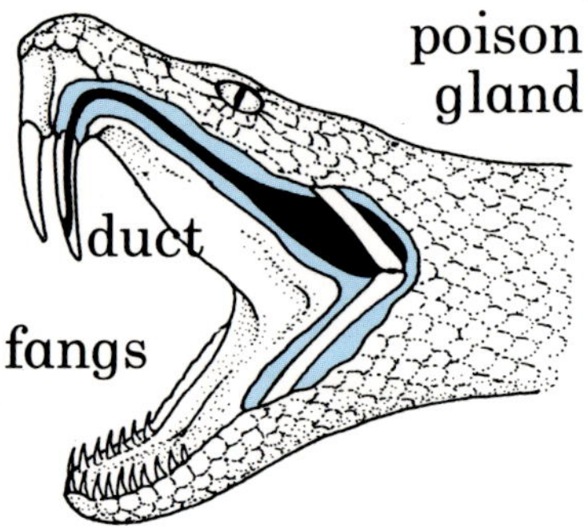

The rattlesnake kills its prey by pumping poison into it through long, hollow teeth called fangs. Snakes can open their mouths amazingly wide, and they swallow their prey whole. A large snake can even swallow a pig!

The tiger

The tiger, like most cats, **stalks** its prey slowly and quietly. Its claws are hidden inside its big, soft paws. The tiger makes very little noise as it creeps towards its prey. When it gets within about 20 metres, the tiger bounds forward at high speed and leaps onto the prey. It sticks its sharp

claws into the animal. Then the tiger uses its big teeth to kill the prey. Tigers feed mainly on wild pigs, deer and antelopes.

Mussel 'soup'

The starfish is a sea creature with hundreds of sucker-like feet. It eats mussels and other shellfish. It opens their shells by pulling them apart with its suckers. Then it pushes its stomach into the shells. Juices from the stomach dissolve the soft parts of the prey and the starfish drinks the 'soup'.

▲ The golden eagle is a bird of prey. It catches rabbits, hares and various kinds of birds. It tears off their flesh with its sharp, hooked beak.

◄ The tiger creeps up quietly on its prey before making the kill.

Drilling for food

Some sea snails use special teeth to drill through mussel shells. Then they pour digestive juices into the holes and suck out the 'soup'.

Trappers

Many animals chase their prey, but others wait for the prey to come to them. Some animals have special lures or baits to attract their prey. Others set traps.

Ambushers

Some animals are ambushers. They lie in wait for their prey. The chameleon lizard waits motionless in trees and bushes. It catches insects with its long, sticky tongue. This lizard looks like its surroundings, so the insects don't notice it. Sea anemones look like plants, but their deadly **tentacles** catch any

▲ A chameleon can change colour to match different backgrounds, so it is not always easy to see.

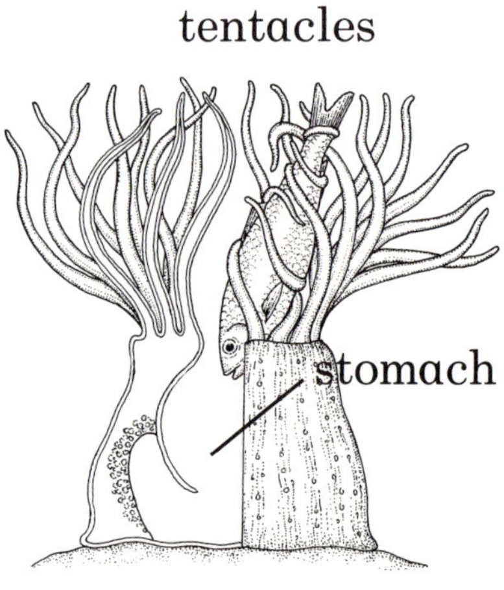

▲ This sea anemone has killed a fish with the poisonous darts on its tentacles. It is pushing the fish into its stomach to be digested.

▲ The angler-fish swallows any fish that tries to eat the bait hanging from a spine on its head.

small animal that happens to bump into them.

Trappers

The alligator snapping turtle sits in the water with its mouth open. It waggles its pink, worm-like tongue. This attracts small fish. When they are close, the turtle snaps them up. The angler-fish lures other fish to their deaths with a flap of skin dangling just above its mouth. This acts like bait on a fishing rod. Many spiders make a web from sticky silk. This traps insects that fly into the web. The spider kills them with a poisonous bite and eats them.

▲ An insect called an ant-lion digs a sandy pit and buries itself at the bottom. Its huge jaws grab ants and other small insects that fall into the pit.

Plant Eaters

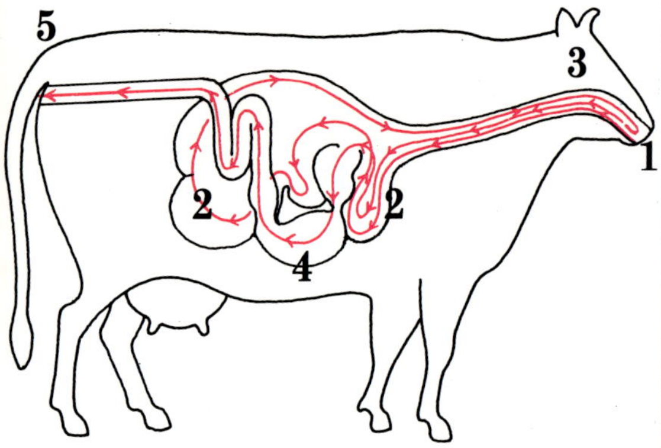

▲ The cow eats food (**1**). This is stored in the stomach (**2**). The food returns to the mouth for chewing (**3**). After the food is digested (**4**), the remaining waste passes out of the body (**5**).

Animals that eat only plants are called herbivores. They can find food almost anywhere. Besides leaves, they may eat seeds, fruit, roots, or even tree bark. Some herbivores drink tree sap.

Chewing the cud

Leaves are hard to digest. So animals that feed mainly on grass and other leaves need special digestive systems. Cows, sheep, giraffes, antelopes and deer have a large and complicated stomach to deal with their food. At first, the unchewed food is stored in a part of the stomach called the rumen. Later, the animal brings up the food and chews it thoroughly. This is called chewing the cud. The chewed food then goes to another part of

Fancy that!

Sun-birds feed mainly on nectar, which they suck from flowers with their long, slender beaks.

▶ These animals are all herbivores living together on the African grasslands. Each kind of animal eats different plants.

the stomach, ready for the final stages of **digestion**.

Living together

Various herbivores can live together because they eat different kinds of plants. Some graze on grasses and other short plants. Other herbivores eat from trees and bushes.

Did you know?

▼ Black and white rhinos look similar. But their lips differ because they eat different foods. The black rhino browses on bushes and the white rhino feeds on grass.

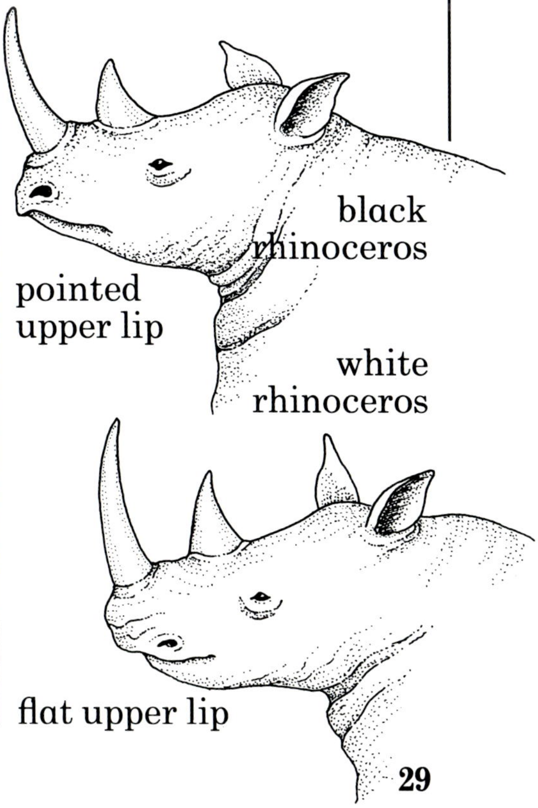

Versatile Eaters

► Rats eat almost anything. Hungry rats will even chew candle wax and the plastic coverings of electric cables.

▼ Dung beetles collect balls of dung. They bury the dung and eat it later.

Animals that eat both plants and other animals are called omnivores. We are omnivores, and so are chimps, bears, pigs and blackbirds. Chimps feed mainly on fruit, but they also eat termites and other insects. They may even kill and eat baby baboons and antelopes.

Omnivores

Animals that aren't fussy about their food can survive almost anywhere. Foxes hunt other animals in the countryside, but they can live just as well in towns. There they find plenty of scraps of food in dustbins.

Scavengers

Many animals feed on the dead bodies and dung of other creatures. We call these animals **scavengers**. They are important animals because they prevent rubbish from building up.

▲ Vultures feed on dead animals. They leave only the bones.

◀ Chimpanzees catch termites by dipping twigs into the termites' nests.

A Strict Diet

Some animals eat special foods, such as blood and tiny specks of plant and animal material. To eat foods like this, the animals have unusual mouth parts.

Blood drinkers

Some animals feed on the blood of other creatures. They include vampire bats, leeches and mosquitoes. Their mouths are specially adapted for cutting their victims. Blood normally

Vampire bat

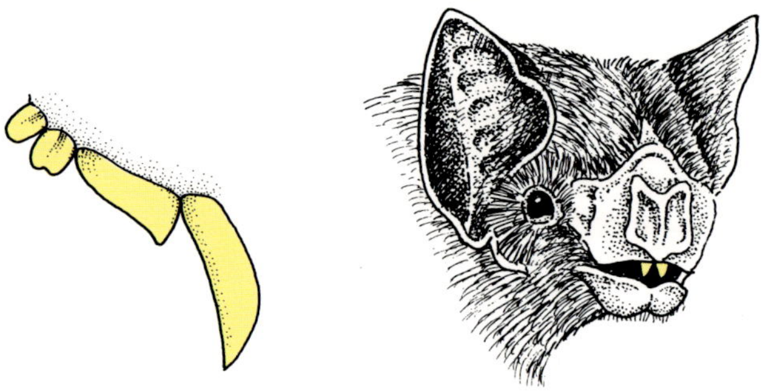

sharp upper teeth (incisors)

► The vampire bat uses its razor-sharp teeth to bite its victims. Then it laps up the blood. The bat does not kill its victims. But it may infect them with the deadly disease called rabies.

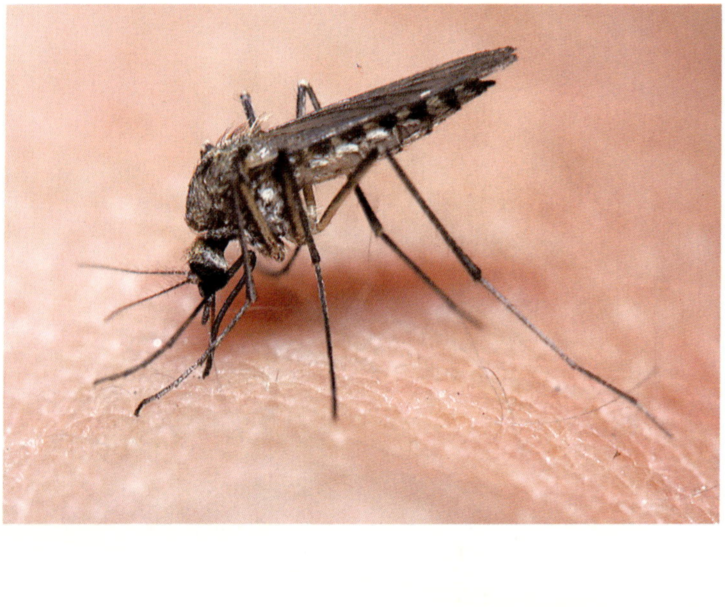

► The female mosquito pricks its victims and sucks their blood. Its mouth is like a hollow needle. Some mosquitoes spread malaria and other diseases.

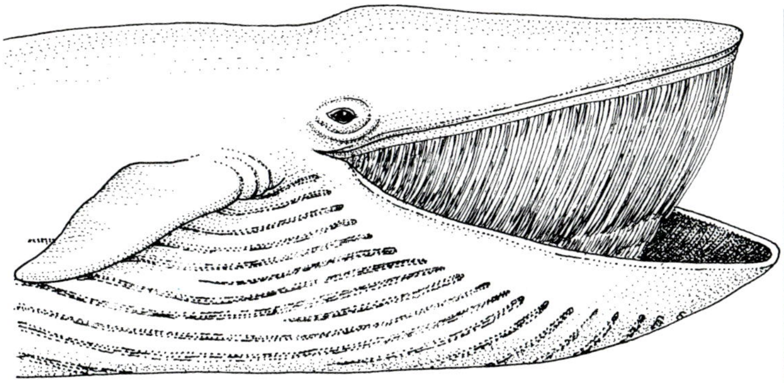

◀ The baleen whale uses a curtain-like screen of a horny substance called baleen to strain tiny animals from the water.

clots quickly and seals up a wound. But the blood drinkers have **saliva** that contains special chemicals. These stop the clotting and keep the blood flowing.

Filter feeders

Many creatures feed by filtering tiny plants and animals from the water. Cockles and mussels feed in this way. They pump water through their bodies and strain food from it.

Some baleen whales are the biggest animals in the sea. Yet they feed on small shrimp-like creatures called krill. Instead of teeth, these whales have sheets of horny baleen hanging from their jaws. They use the baleen to strain the krill from the water.

Did you know?

The giant panda lives in the bamboo forests of China. It feeds mainly on bamboo. Each front foot has an extra 'thumb', specially evolved for holding the bamboo. But much of the bamboo forest in China is dying. This is making it hard for the pandas there to get enough food.

Defence

Animals have many ways of protecting themselves from their predators. Many animals have special colours and shapes that blend in with their surroundings. This is called camouflage. It makes the animals hard to see. Some fishes and other creatures can even change colour to match different backgrounds.

Shells and spines

Snails and turtles retreat into their strong shells when they are attacked. Then they are quite

▲ Stick insects look like twigs, so their enemies don't notice them.

summer plumage

► The ptarmigan turns white to match the winter snow.

safe. Porcupines and hedgehogs are covered with sharp spines. So other animals rarely dare to attack them.

Poisons and stings

Many animals taste nasty, and some have poisonous bites or stings for protection. Some such animals, which include frogs, snakes and wasps, have bright colours and bold patterns. Their predators learn to recognize these markings and so they leave the animals alone.

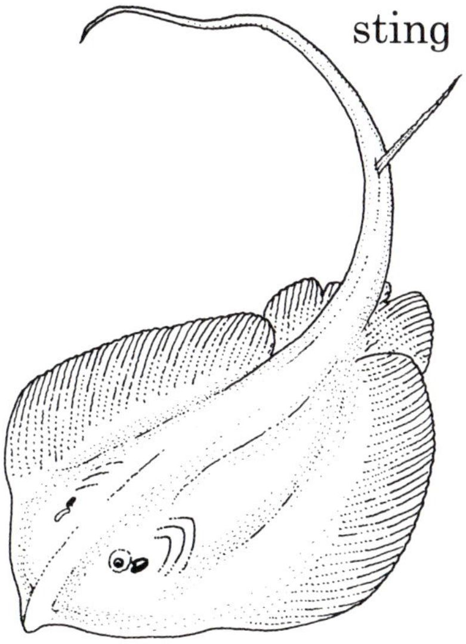

▲ The sting-ray defends itself with the poisonous spine on its tail.

Survival trick

A lizard can break off its tail if attacked. Its predator gets the wriggling tail, but the lizard escapes. It then grows a new tail.

CHAPTER FOUR

THE SENSES

Eyes

Many **invertebrate** animals have simple eyes and can only tell light from darkness. Insects have compound eyes. These sometimes contain thousands of tiny lenses.

Vertebrate animals have eyes like ours, but they don't all see things in the way that we do. Brightly coloured birds and fishes can usually see colours, but most mammals cannot. For example, dogs and rabbits see everything in black, white and various shades of grey.

▲ The dragonfly's huge compound eyes can spot any movement around it.

► A bird's eye, first as we see it and then as a bee sees it. Each of the bee's tiny lenses produces a separate image.

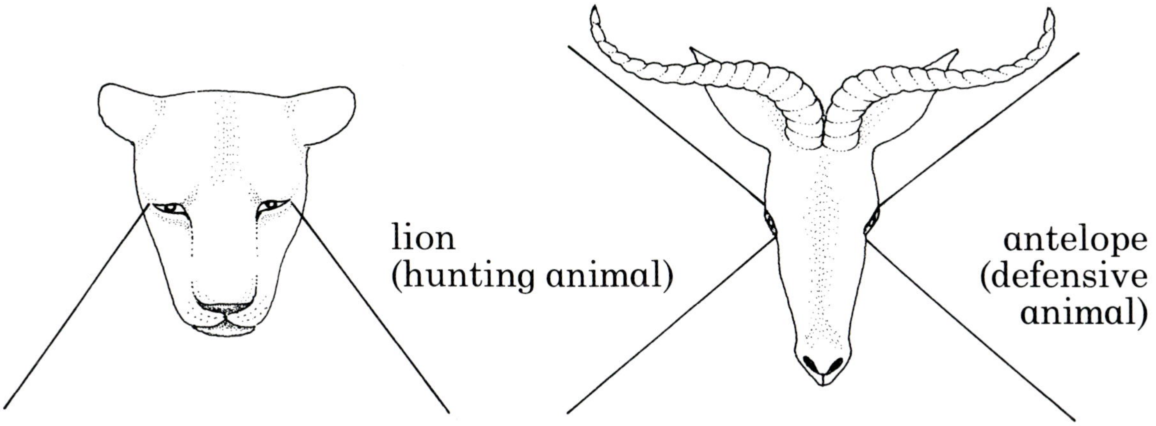

Eye positions

Looking at animals' eyes can tell us a lot about how they live. Hunting animals have eyes at the front of the head, for judging the distance to their prey. Plant-eating animals, such as deer and antelopes, have eyes at the sides of the head. So they can see to the sides and to the front. This helps them to spot an attack coming from almost any direction.

▲ The lion has a narrow field of vision to concentrate on its prey. But the antelope can see over a wide area to spot attackers.

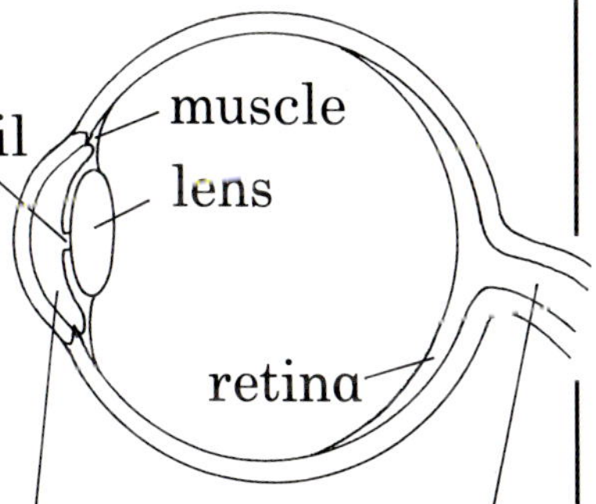

▲ Light enters the eye of a vertebrate animal through the pupil. The lens helps to focus an image onto the retina at the back. The retina sends signals along the optic nerve to the brain. These signals tell the brain what the eye sees.

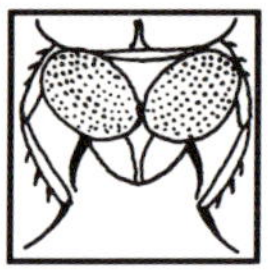

Smell and Taste

▲ The wolf's sense of smell is 100 times better than ours.

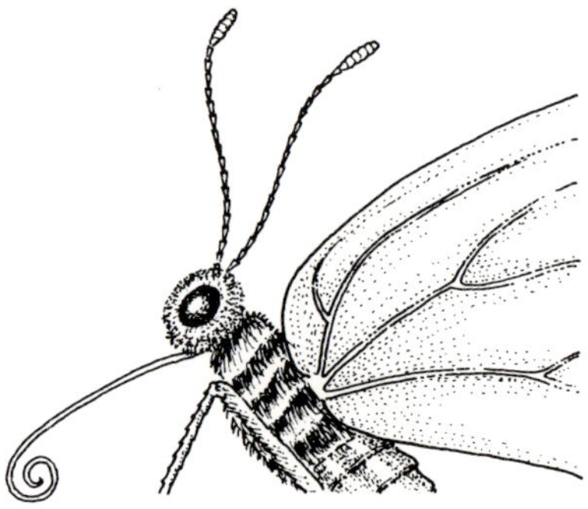

► Many male moths have large antennae, or feelers, to pick up the females' scents.

Animals use the nose and other organs to detect tiny chemical particles in the air or water. These particles are called smells or scents. Tastes are similar to smells, but they can be picked up only by touching substances with the tongue or other taste organs.

A smelly world

The world is full of smells. These can tell animals a lot about their surroundings. Many animals find their food by following smells. Sharks can smell the blood of an injured animal more than five kilometres (three miles) away. Salmon use their sense of smell to find their way about.

◀ This male lion has just picked up the scent of a female that is ready to mate. He will soon track her down and start courting her.

Scent for signals

Animal scents often act as messages for their neighbours. Special glands, often near the eye or under the tail, give out strong-smelling liquids. These are left on the ground or on plants to mark out **territories**. The scents warn other animals to keep away. Many female animals give off special smells to tell the males that they are ready to mate.

Did you know?

A snake flicks out its tongue to pick up scent particles. Then it puts them on the Jacobson's organ at the back of its mouth. This sends smell signals to the brain.

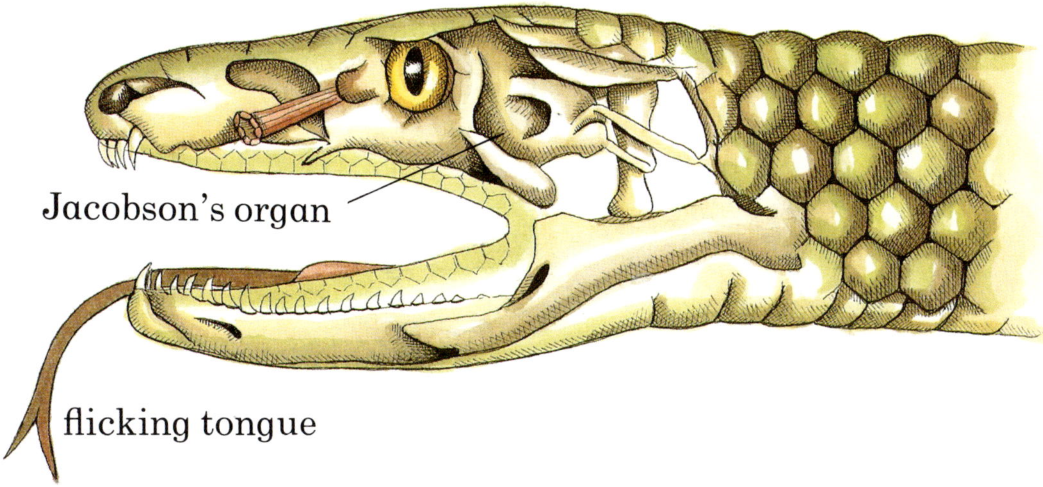

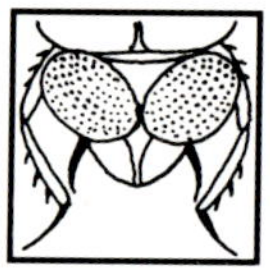

Hearing and Touch

► The bush-baby uses its eyes and ears to detect food and danger.

Did you know?

Snakes have no ears, so the rattle-snake can't hear the noise it makes when it rattles its tail. It does this to warn other animals to keep away. Snakes can feel vibrations in the ground.

Hearing and touch are important senses for many animals. Forest-dwellers can't see far through the trees, so they must listen for their enemies. Most **mammals** have large, movable ear-flaps. These can pick up sounds from all directions. Animals that go about at night also have good hearing. They often use their ears to find food as well as to listen for enemies.

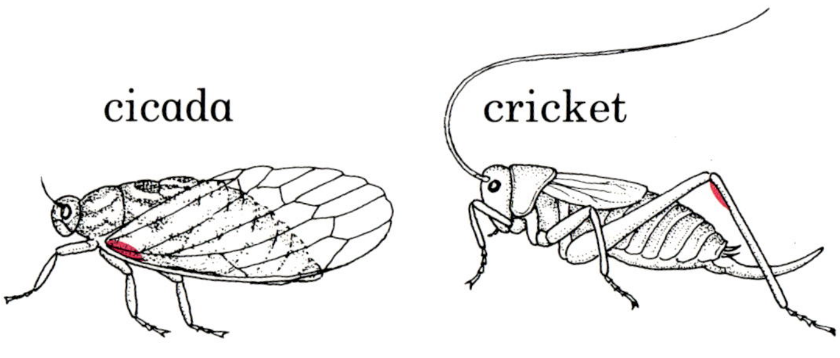

hearing organs

► Cicadas have ears near the base of their wings. Crickets have tiny ears on their legs.

Touch

Almost all parts of our bodies are sensitive to touch, but we can feel things best with our finger-tips. They are packed with special **nerves** called touch receptors. Many mammals have whiskers that are sensitive to the slightest touch. These usually help the animals to feel their way in the dark. Many insects use their **antennae** to feel their way about.

▼ These animals live on or near the sea-bed. The water there is often cloudy. Crabs and lobsters use their antennae to feel their way around. The catfish has growths called barbels around its mouth. And the gurnard has finger-like growths under its head. The fishes use these sensitive parts to search for food in the sand.

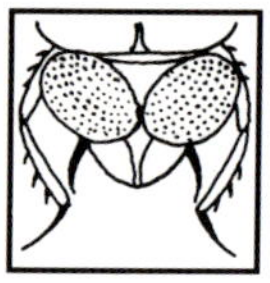

Special Sensors

Sight, hearing, touch, smell and taste are the five main senses. But animals have some other ways of exploring their world.

Electric sensors

Some fish make electricity in their bodies and send it as a current through the water. Nearby objects cause the strength of the current to change. The fishes can detect these

lateral line (magnified)

tiny hairs pick up movement in the water

► Fishes have a line along each side of the body. These are called lateral lines. They consist of little pockets of jelly containing tiny hairs. The hairs pick up vibrations and tell the fish what is happening in the surrounding water.

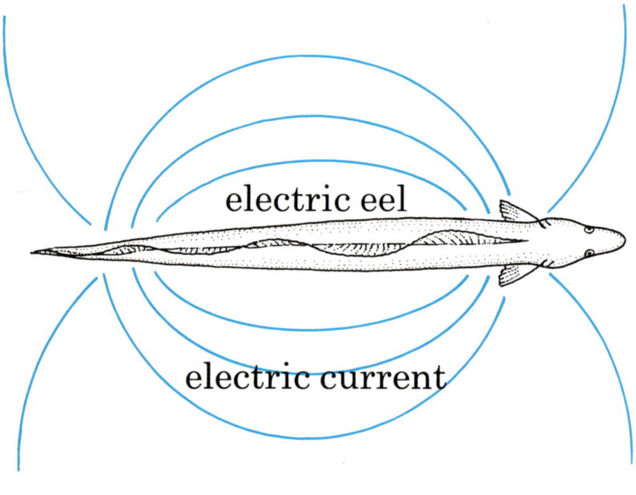

► The electric eel produces a powerful current. This is used to kill prey and stun enemies and for guidance.

◀ Pit vipers have a heat-sensitive pit near each eye. The pits detect small temperature changes caused by other animals nearby. This is how pit vipers find the mice and other small animals that they eat.

changes. So they know when another fish is near.

Heat sensors

Rattlesnakes and other pit vipers can sense the body heat of other animals. This helps them to follow and catch prey in the dark.

Echo-location

Night-flying bats give out high-pitched sounds. And they listen to the echoes that bounce back from nearby objects. The echoes tell the bats where things are, so they don't bump into them. This system is called echo-location. ▼

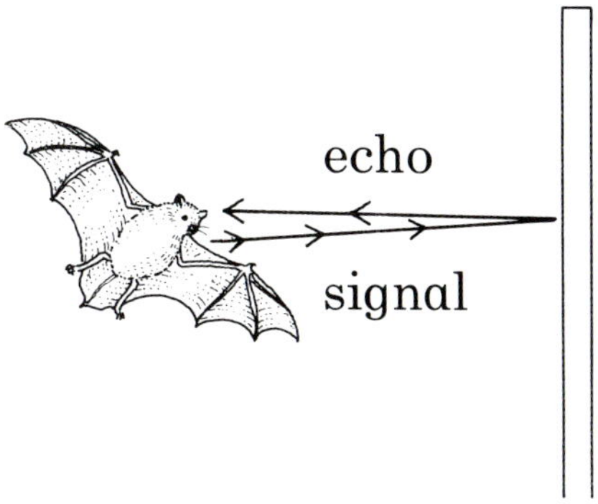

CHAPTER FIVE

REPRODUCTION

How Animals Reproduce

All animals must reproduce to continue their species. Tiny creatures like the amoeba just split into two. Each half then becomes a complete new animal. Larger animals usually produce young by sexual reproduction.

Sexual reproduction

Most animals are either males or females. The males produce **sperms** and the females produce eggs. An egg can grow into a new animal, but only after a male sperm has entered it. This process is called **fertilization**. It usually happens inside the female's body after mating. Some water animals scatter sperms and eggs into the water, and fertilization takes place there.

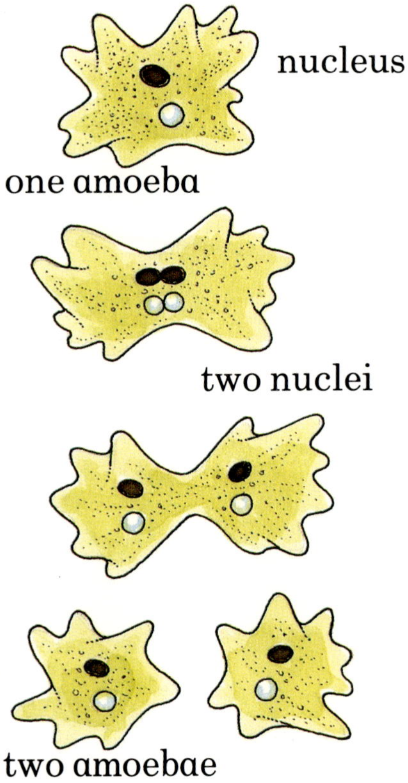

▲ The amoeba reproduces by dividing into two.

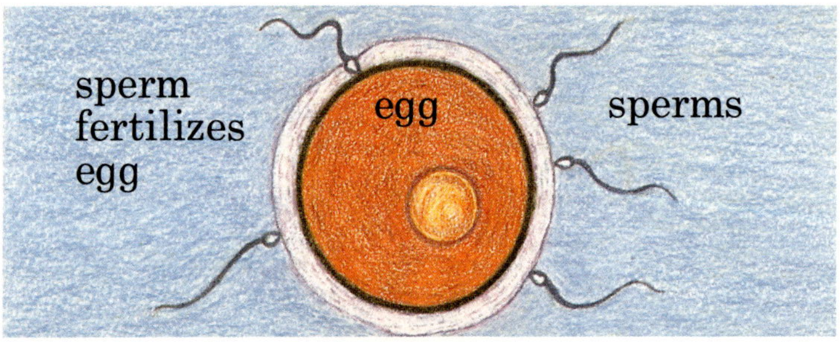

► Eggs are much bigger than sperms. But only one sperm is needed to fertilize the egg. Then it will grow into a baby.

Eggs and young

Birds and many other animals lay their eggs when they have been fertilized. Each egg contains a supply of food for the young animal growing inside it. Most mammals don't lay eggs. The fertilized eggs grow into babies inside the mother's body. The babies get food from the mother's blood stream. The mother gives birth to the young after a few weeks or months. Then she feeds them on her milk until they are able to eat solid foods.

Facts and feats

- Emperor penguins hold their one egg on their feet to keep it warm.
- Pandas weigh only about 150 grams at birth. But, after just eight weeks, they weigh about 3 kilograms.
- Kangaroo babies are very tiny when they are born. They spend several months growing in the mother's pouch.
- A baby elephant grows for 22 months in its mother's womb.
- The only mammals that lay eggs are the duck-billed platypus and the echidna.

◀ These lions are mating. The male's sperms will fertilize the female's eggs. These will then grow into cubs inside her body. The cubs will be born about 15 weeks after mating.

Finding a Mate

Amazing but true

► Male bower birds attract females with displays of coloured objects. They use bright stones and items such as buttons, bottle caps and plastic scrap.

▼ This peacock's display will attract a female for mating.

Show-offs

Birds, fish and many other animals use bright colours to attract their mates. It is usually the male that is colourful, and he shows off in front of the female. Peacocks display their great fans of feathers. The females, called peahens, choose the most colourful males. Many birds also sing to attract their mates, and so do grasshoppers.

Dancers

Male and female cranes dance together and leap into the air when **courting**. Male newts dance in front of the females.

The females are attracted by the dance and by the red underbelly of the males. Even scorpions dance, holding each other with their pincers.

Animal flash-lights

Fireflies, which are actually beetles, flash lights to attract each other. Some deep-sea fish also use lights. Each species uses a different pattern of flashes.

Wedding presents

Male adelie penguins give pebbles to the females before mating. Some male spiders give flies to their mates.

▼ Newts and lizards get more colour at breeding time. The male green lizard shows off his blue throat by bobbing his head up and down. Scorpions dance before mating.

Caring Parents

Most fishes, frogs and insects lay their eggs and then take no more interest in their young. Many other animals care for their eggs and young for a long time.

Looking after eggs

Female crabs carry their eggs under their bodies, protected by flaps of hard shell. Wolf spiders carry their eggs in silken bags. Some fish, called mouth-brooders, carry their eggs in their mouth. Animals that protect their eggs don't have to lay so many in order to produce young. For the eggs have a better chance of survival if the parents are protective.

► The female orang-utan spends a lot of time caring for her baby. She protects it and teaches it how to find food and to survive in the forest.

▼ The male midwife toad carries the female's eggs on his back legs. He takes them to the water when they are ready to hatch.

◀ When a baby kangaroo is born, it crawls into its mother's pouch. It stays there, feeding on milk, until it is big enough to look after itself. Animals with pouches for their babies are called marsupials. Wombats, bandicoots, koalas and opossums are all marsupials.

Birds and mammals

Birds look after their eggs and keep them warm – usually in cosy nests. Baby pheasants and ducks can walk and feed themselves as soon as they hatch. But many baby birds are helpless. They are cared for in the nest.

Baby mammals all feed on the mother's milk. Some mammals are blind and helpless at birth. So they have to be looked after for weeks, or even months. Baby antelopes and deer can walk when they are only an hour old. But they must still stay near their mothers, who give them milk.

▼ The female crocodile carries her newly hatched babies to the river in her mouth. This looks rather dangerous for the babies, but she is very gentle with them.

Changes

Some baby animals look very different from their parents. A butterfly spends its early life as a caterpillar. Adult mussels and barnacles are fixed to rocks. But their young are tiny **larvae** that drift freely in the sea. The larvae turn into adults when they settle on the rocks.

The plaice

A newly-hatched plaice looks like most other young fish. But, after a few days, its left eye moves over to the right side. The fish then becomes very flat. It swims on its left side, with both eyes looking up towards the surface.

▼ Many sea creatures have larvae that look very different from the adults. Here are a starfish and a crab with their larvae. The larvae float in the sea. There are also millions of very tiny animals and plants in the sea. These are called plankton.

Did you know?

◀ Tadpoles are the larvae of frogs. Like fishes, tadpoles breathe with gills. Gradually, they lose their gills and develop lungs. And they grow two pairs of legs. Then they move onto the land as young frogs.

Nymphs

Dragonflies and mayflies lay their eggs in water. Their young are called **nymphs**. Wings slowly grow on their backs. When the nymphs are fully grown, they leave the water. Then they break out of their old skins and fly away.

CHAPTER SIX

COMMUNITIES

Herds and Flocks

Antelopes usually live in large herds on the wide open grasslands. They are much safer in herds because there are more eyes and ears to watch for enemies. Many other grazing animals live in herds. Some of these herds are family groups, with just a few parents and their young. But other herds may contain thousands of animals.

Flocks

Some birds also form huge flocks, especially in winter. Thousands of starlings often gather to sleep in the same tree or on a building.

▼ Wolves live in packs. These are often large family groups, with several parents and all their youngsters. The wolves hunt together and help each other to rear their young.

▲ Wildebeeste, zebras and impalas all live in herds on the African plains. They find it safer to stay together.

Breeding

Elephant seals spend most of their lives at sea. But, at breeding time, they gather on certain beaches. The strongest male on each beach chases the other males away. Then he mates with all the females.

Male deer also fight over their females in the breeding season. They wrestle using their antlers. Then the winners round up groups of females for mating. Outside the breeding season, the females live in herds with their young. The males live separately.

▼ These female elephant seals are part of one male's breeding group.

Colonies

Some animals live in very close groups, where each member works for the good of the whole colony. Chacma baboons live in groups of up to 80 animals. Each group is ruled by one or more big males. Younger males guard the edges of the group. They fight off leopards and other enemies.

Bees, wasps and ants

Honey-bees live in colonies containing three kinds of bees. The queen bee lays all the eggs. And she controls the colony by giving out scents that keep the other bees contented. Most of the

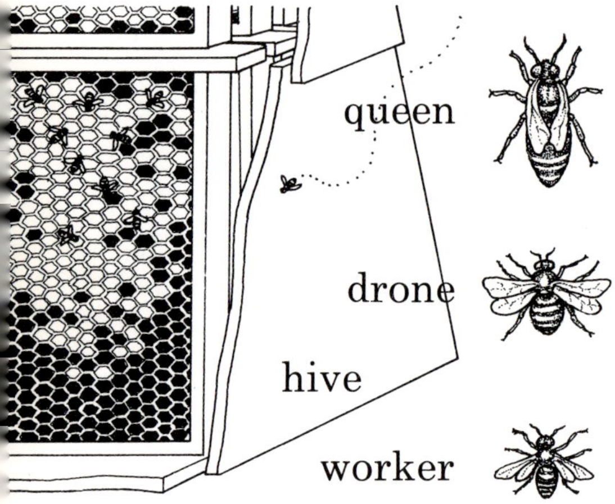

▲ The three kinds of honey-bee. There may be thousands of workers in a hive.

► Baboons love to groom each other. This helps to keep the group together. The baboon by himself is looking out for danger.

bees are workers. They build the nest and collect food for the younger bees. Male bees, called drones, do no work. They mate with new queens in the summer.

Wasps and ants also live in colonies. Some ant colonies are guarded by soldier ants. They use their strong jaws to fight enemies.

Corals
Coral colonies are made up of thousands of tiny animals called polyps. They are all joined and they share their food.

◀ This coral colony is made up of thousands of animals like tiny sea anemones.

The Portuguese man-of-war

▼ This weird animal is a colony of many kinds of animals called polyps. Each kind has its own job. Some form the food-catching tentacles, while others digest the food. They all hang from the float, which is a very large polyp.

Partners

Some animals form partnerships with other species. Some partnerships help both partners, while others help only one.

Helpful friends

Ants and aphids help each other. The aphids make a sugary liquid called honeydew that the ants like to drink. In return, the ants fight off some of the aphids' enemies, such as ladybirds.

Small sea fish, called cleaners, nibble dead skin and parasites from larger fish. The cleaners get food and the larger fish are cleaned. So both animals benefit.

Clownfish avoid their enemies by sheltering among the **tentacles** of giant sea anemones. In return for the shelter, the anemones get scraps of the fish's food.

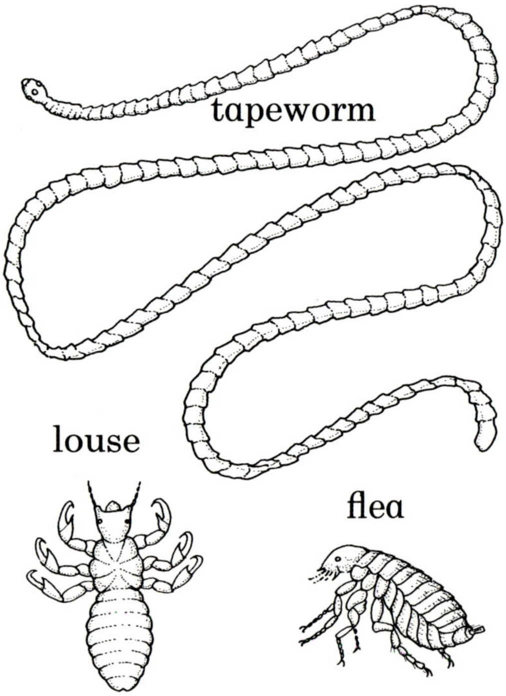

▲ These animals are parasites. The tapeworm lives inside other animals and soaks up food. The louse and the flea suck blood.

► These ants are drinking sweet honeydew from aphids.

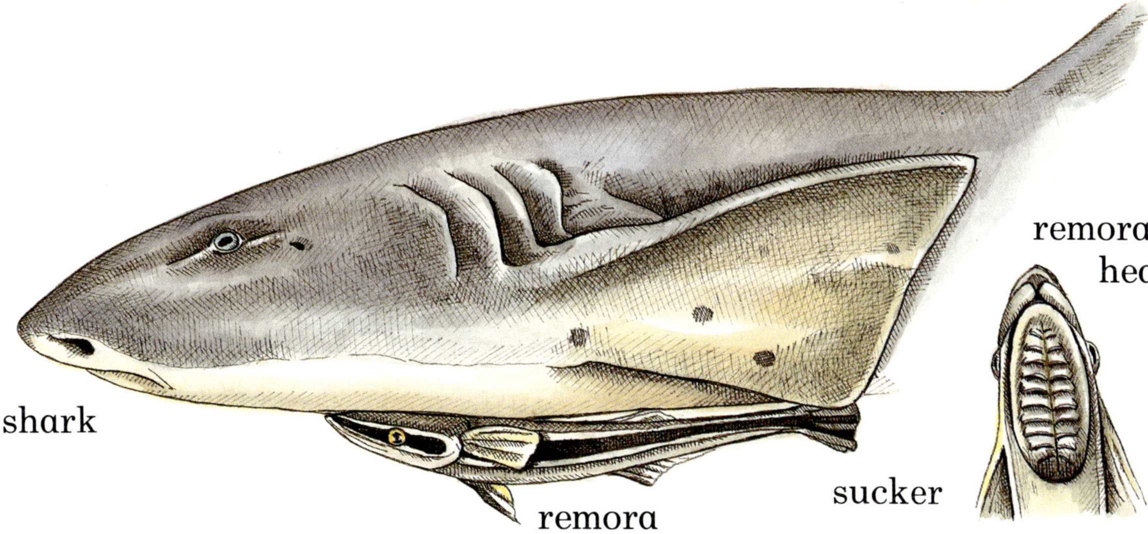

Uninvited guests

Some animals take food or protection from their partners, but give nothing back. Ragworms live in the shells of hermit crabs and steal bits of the crab's food. The crabs get nothing in return, but they are not harmed in any way by the ragworms.

▲ The remora is a weird fish that attaches itself to sharks. It sticks on, using the large sucker on its head. The remora gets a free ride and may also get scraps of the shark's food. But it does not harm the shark.

Parasites actually harm their partners, by sucking blood or attacking other parts of their bodies. But they don't usually kill their partners, for this would cut off their food supplies.

◀ These clownfish are quite safe with giant sea anemones for partners. The anemones' stinging tentacles don't harm the clownfish. But they keep away the enemies of the clownfish.

Messages

► These butterfly fish recognise each other by their markings.

▲ Roe deer warn their companions of danger by flashing their white rumps.

People talk to each other to pass on information. Scientists have found that whales and dolphins also talk to each other regularly, although we don't understand their language. Birds sing to attract mates and to defend their territories. And they also have special calls to warn each other when enemies appear. Many other animals **communicate** with scent, colours or special body movements.

▼ By using special microphones, scientists have found that killer whales talk to each other nearly all the time.

Who goes there?

A shoal of fish usually contains just one kind of fish. The fish keep together because they recognize the group's colours and patterns. Animals living in groups often recognize their leaders by their special colours.

Moods

Monkeys and apes use many facial expressions. Each one shows a particular mood. A monkey may yawn, but this doesn't mean that it is tired. It is showing its teeth to threaten another monkey. Wolves and dogs also signal to each other with facial expressions.

▲ This male mandrill is the leader of his troop. The other mandrills recognize him by his bright face.

Territories

Animals have many ways of warning rivals to stay away from their territories. Birds sing, gibbons shout, and many animals spray urine around.

Good news

◀ Honey-bees that have found good food perform a wriggly dance when they get back to the hive. The dance tells the other bees where to find the food.

Glossary

Antennae: a word used to describe a long thin feeler found on the heads of insects and other animals, such as crabs, used for smelling and touching.

Burrow: this is a hole in the ground which is dug by some animals for shelter.

Clot: when you cut yourself your blood thickens and forms a lump which blocks the wound and stops you from bleeding any more. This thickening of the blood is called a clot.

Communicate: a word used to mean that information is passing from one animal to another. People can communicate by talking, whilst animals can communicate by smell, colour or special body movements.

Courting: this word describes the way animals attract each other when looking for a mate. For instance, the male peacock displays its beautiful tail to attract the female peahen.

Denser: this means that an object is thicker or heavier than another object. For example, a block of metal is denser than a sponge that is the same size.

Digestion: the process by which food is broken down in the stomach and gut and is made useful to the body.

Evolution: this word is used to describe the gradual change over millions of years of living things from simple early forms to the more complex present-day forms.

Fertilization: when the male and female reproductive parts of a plant or animal meet, fertilization takes place. A new animal or plant then starts to grow.

Flippers: these are limbs of an animal that are used when swimming. The seal has flippers instead of arms and hands.

Fossil: traces of past life forms that have been kept safe in ancient rocks.

Hibernation: some animals become very sleepy during the winter when there is little food around. This inactivity is called hibernation.

Invertebrate: an animal without a backbone.

Jet propulsion: this is a word that describes a way of moving very quickly. For example, the squid squirts water from its body at a terrific speed and so sends itself off in the opposite direction from the way the water went.

Larvae: the grub form of an insect, from the time it leaves the egg until it changes into an adult insect.

Mammals: warm-blooded animals that feed their young on their own milk.

Nerves: all animals have wire-like tubes that carry around messages. If you cut yourself, your nerve will carry a message to your brain saying that it hurts.

Nymphs: the young form of some insects that resembles the adult insect but with wings and other parts not yet fully grown.

Organs: parts of an animal or plant that do one particular job. For instance, the heart is the organ that pumps blood around the body.

Predators: this word is used to describe animals that live by hunting other animals for food.

Prehensile: this word describes

something that is able to grip like a hand; for example, a monkey's tail.

Prey: an animal that is killed and eaten by another animal, the predator.

Reptiles: cold-blooded animals with scaly skin.

Saliva: this is a liquid that is produced in the mouth which helps to break down the food you eat and make it useful to the body.

Scavengers: animals that feed on the dead bodies and dung of other animals. Vultures are scavengers.

Species: this is a word used to describe a particular type of animal or plant. Lions are a species.

Sperm: sex cells made by males and used in the process of fertilization and sexual reproduction.

Stalks: this is a word used to describe a hunter who approaches its victim quietly so that the victim does not realise that it is being hunted.

Streamlined: a word that means an animal is a good shape for going through air or water. A dolphin is streamlined.

Tentacles: a word used to describe bendy arm-like features that are used for grasping. Octopuses have tentacles.

Territories: areas of land that are the home of one animal or a group of animals. Territories are claimed by animals and then ruled by them. They are always fiercely guarded.

Tropical: a word that describes very hot and wet areas of land.

Veins: tubes in an animal that carry blood around the body to the heart. In an insects's wing, veins are hollow, slender tubes used for strengthening and support.

Vertebrates: animals without backbones.

Index

A number in **bold** shows that the entry is illustrated on that page. The same page often has writing about the entry too.